D1826571

DOMESTIC
FUGUES

DOMESTIC FUGUES

RICHARD NEWMAN

STEEL TOE BOOKS

BOWLING GREEN, KENTUCKY

Copyright © 2009 Richard Newman
All rights reserved.

ISBN 978-0-9824169-1-4

STEEL TOE BOOKS
Western Kentucky University
Department of English
1906 College Heights Blvd. #11086
Bowling Green, KY 42101-1086
steeltoebooks.com

COVER ART
Jan Verkolje, Dutch, 1650-1693
A Gallant Musical Pause at Delft, 1674
Oil on canvas
38 1/8 x 31 1/8 in. (96.8 x 79.1 cm.)
Purchase, Museum Art Fund, 1958.3
Collection of The Speed Art Museum,
Louisville, Kentucky

AUTHOR PHOTOGRAPH
Robert George

COVER AND BOOK DESIGN
Molly McCaffrey

For my girls, Kara and Natalie

fugue \fügue\ *n* [prob. fr. It *fuga* flight, fugue, fr. L, flight, fr. *fugere*] (1597) **1** : a polyphonic musical composition in which one or two themes are repeated or imitated by successively entering voices and contrapuntally developed in a continuous interweaving of the voice parts **2** : a disturbed state of consciousness in which the one affected performs acts of which he appears to be conscious but of which on recovery he has no recollection

—*Webster's Ninth New Collegiate Dictionary*

CONTENTS

ONE

Old Bird 3

Domestic Fugues 4

    1. Bathtub
    2. The New Math
    3. Showertime
    4. Sunday Fugue
    5. Empty House
    6. Moving Portraits
    7. Short December Fugue

The Final Fuck 11

Trap 13

Man Drives with Shark Attached to Leg 14

Wharf-Ruins 16

The Unborn 17

Centipedes 18

Dog Days 21

T W O

Five Songs for Hidden Places   25

     1. Song for the Cool Spot of my Pillow
     2. Matchbook Song
     3. Back of a Beer Label
     4. Back Alley Song
     5. Solitary Drinking Song

Home   31

Delay   32

Church   33

Sweet November   35

Horse   36

Soulard Mardi Gras Round   38

Insestina   39

Bless Their Hearts   41

May All Your Christmases Be White-Knuckled   42

THREE

The Artists   47

Two Lullabies   49

       1. After Drinking
       2. Falling Asleep

Fugue in Cold and Rain   52

Flood Watch   53

While You Were Away . . .   54

Lessons from the Garden   56

Gifts   58

The White Bus of Failure   60

Dumpster Fires   61

December Evening   62

Communion   63

When Men Stopped Wearing Hats,   64
When Women Stopped Wearing Gloves

Little Fugue of Love and Death   65

ONE

OLD BIRD

His old Impala burned more oil than gas,
slowing traffic back to the exit ramp,
and I saw as it finally came my turn to pass,
sticking through the window, a stump—
his arm rounded off above the elbow
and wrapped up in the long, cool highway wind—
and bobbing on his shoulder, all bright yellow
and red, a rooster. The man turned and grinned
as we traveled, even, between tall green seas
of cornstalks that threatened to crash over the road.
His rooster's feathers fluttered in the breeze.
Through his farm-dusted windshield, the bird glowed.
And though it took me miles to understand,
he'd raised his arm—a friendly wave of his hand.

DOMESTIC FUGUES

1. Bathtub

A black snake in our bathtub
before I turn on water—
a long bright shadow writhing.
How on earth did it get in?
Its dry skin brushes and rubs
against the dry porcelain.
It searches rounded corners,
banishing thoughts of bathing.

How the hell did it get in
the belly of our clawfoot?
It coils around the drain,
keeps looking for luck's way out,
and strains to reach the rim.
Our hatred is instinctive—
how on earth did it get in—
Christ! I can't let this thing live.

This long bright shadow that writhes
then coils around the drain,
a ripple of black water—
we are the two of us trapped
by a piqued shadow of nature,
and I stand repulsed and rapt,
but the only out is death
for the snake trapped in our bath.

2. The New Math

The furnace groans in the basement,
and the whole house shudders with heat,
dissolving even the dog's dreams.
Drowsy mathematicians,
we find lost hours from the week
before to make our sleepy sums,
having stayed up all night fighting.
Everything adds up to nothing.

Snowflakes tap against the windows,
the world outside us nothing more
than a muffled drift of itself.
Inside we hear the furnace groan
the whole house awake, shuddering.
The cold bedspace stretched between us—
this is not the dream we once dreamed,
all night fighting about nothing—

the night before, our angry sums,
nothings add up to everything.
Now we drift in and out of sleep
and shudder beneath the covers.
Two floors below, the furnace groans.
Snowflakes tap against dark windows
dreaming the whole world will add up.
Even a dog can have his dreams.

3. Showertime

Wash rinse repeat wash rinse repeat wash rinse,
I bend beneath a full head of steam.
Our words replay, a loop to make me wince,
wash rinse repeat wash rinse repeat wash rinse,
shower pounding tension into past tense.
I could stand in here all day and daydream
(wash rinse repeat wash rinse repeat wash rinse)
unbending beneath a full head of steam.

4. Sunday Fugue

The phone rings—we don't answer.
We rustle bills, scratch pens.
As if from a gravel shore
we watch ourselves move
beneath the shadowed water.
Our silence hunkers down
till we can barely breathe.

We watch ourselves move
across the bedroom carpet.
Our silence sharpens its teeth.
The room sweeps light to dark,
and it's too much work to breathe.
All night we work beneath

the hunkering silence, breath
like clothes sluffing in the dark.
Grave silence does its work.
Our silence sharpens its teeth—
we don't dare move or answer.

5. Empty House

Spring pulls us inside
out, the house empty
of voice, rooms empty
of shadows, mirrors
empty of us, empty,
rug empty of dog.
The sink drips happily.
Clocks keep time to themselves.
The phone rings, both stories.
Someone leaves a message:
Where are you? We are
out of the house, empty.
Books snooze on the shelves.
All afternoon a shaft
of sunlight searches
the empty room. Where
are we while clocks keep time
to themselves and the sink
drips happily? We are
inside out, while the wind
from an open window
flutters important papers,
wind empty of voice,
which pulls us back inside.

6. Moving Portraits

The pictures in the hall
smile back from better times.
We pass them, both arms full
of boxes for the move,
try not to knock the frames.
We know fuck-all about love.

The people in the frames
watch us walk back and forth
maybe a hundred times,
dirtying up the hall,
each time more out of breath.
Fuck one more time—for love?—
last time our arms are full.

The faces on the wall
know less than we do now
of love. We know fuck-all.
Each studied back and forth
is one trip closer to death.
We fucked up our love,
but we don't watch or move
the pictures in the hall.

7. Short December Fugue

The roses stain the air
bright crimson up against
the faded grass and fence,
an out of season pair
beneath a curdled sky
while bricks collect the mist.
Strange December roses
I pruned reluctantly
then neglected when you left
now thrive and stain the air
beneath the curdled skies.
No doubt your air is stained
with your own ironies.
Mist thickens into rain.

THE FINAL FUCK

Long after we all know the love is over
we commit recidivism, a ritual.
We may each have found another lover.
This act is more or less mutual.

Is it recidivism or ritual?
One friend was picking up papers from her ex—
the act was more or less mutual.
He'd just let her go. She just wanted sex.

One friend was picking up papers from her ex.
Two others went from courtroom to hotel room.
They couldn't let go, only wanted sex
with each other, like when they were bride and groom.

The two who went from courtroom to hotel room
later threw a big Just Divorced bash.
We shook hands like when they were bride and groom,
brought parting gifts, and toasted them with panache

that night they threw their big Just Divorced bash.
My own ex and I had no such luck,
no parting gifts, no toast, and no panache.
After we sawed through our final fuck,

my soon-to-be-ex and I, who had no luck,
I turned and asked her what the act had meant.
We had just sawn through our final fuck.
She pronounced, "It was an experiment."

I wished I hadn't asked her what she'd meant:
a cadaver wrapped in sheets, cold and pale.
She'd pronounced it an experiment—
an experiment that we both hoped would fail.

Two cadavers wrapped in sheets, cold and pale,
we'd both already found other lovers.
It was an experiment designed to fail,
long after we both knew our love was over.

TRAP

We made the decision in a brittle snap—
and then the long procession of divorce,
chewing ourselves free from a steel trap.

We married in a moment, rash and rapt.
Proving nobody wrong but us, of course,
we made the decision in a brittle snap.

Now sleeplessness and tears are our nightcap,
slow summer nights spent wilting with remorse,
chewing ourselves free from a steel trap,

and that ugly heat—the push, the shove, the slap,
the voice of reason wavering and hoarse
and broken, broken in a brittle snap.

Our child is torn in turn from both our laps.
We try to spare her from the brutal force
required to free ourselves from a steel trap

and take our place among those handicapped
by love, black statistics of legal recourse.
We made the decision with a brittle snap
but chew a lifetime in our steel trap.

Man Drives with Shark Attached to Leg

All morning it ignored my snorkeling—
a Wobbegong, two-foot carpet shark,
moody little bastards, teeth as sharp
as carpet tacks—then out of the blue, pain.
Clamped so tight on my leg I couldn't bleed,
it shook until I gripped its fins and kicked
my way to shore. But I was lucky, could
easily be missing a foot.
On the beach two surfers tried to pry it off
but couldn't break the hundred pounds of pressure
above my knee, so I drove to the clubhouse,
ruing the day I ever bought a stickshift.
When the lifeguards saw me hobble in, one cracked,
"Yeah, my ex-wife wouldn't let go without
taking a piece of me either."
"Sometimes these things attack without reason,"
another said, as if in explanation,
then flushed its gills with fresh water until
its jaws finally fell slack, revealing
two sloppy, bleeding half-arcs, 70
needle-like puncture holes in a bright
constellation of pain. They dropped the shark
in a tank and drove me to the hospital,
and when we returned that night, it was bobbing
belly up against the aerator.
"You want it mounted as a souvenir?"
they asked. I pictured it above my door,
reminding me of life's fierce senselessness,

but I had 70 tiny souvenirs.
I scooped the poor stupid thing from the tank,
carried it like a baby down the beach,
expecting it to wake and bite my arm,
and flung it Olympiad-style over the waves,
white belly flashing in the cold starlight.

WHARF-RUINS

What was our attraction to detritus—
those wharf-ruins with huge, broken wheels,
shattered slabs of cement, ubiquitous
river rats, and knots of rusted steel,
as if the old Ohio had half succeeded
in pounding them back to nature and then gave up.
And why dare gravity, danger signs unheeded,
and climb the crumbling tops, so high a hiccup
or gentle summer breeze could have swept
us off balance on that river-worn bough.
What miseries had we to escape except
perhaps childhood's long, unbearable now,
while dirty brown waves licked the concrete
and puppy whirlpools beckoned at our feet.

THE UNBORN

The sign says *Love your babies, born and unborn.*
Each morning the 40-foot billboard can't be missed,
but know it isn't you—it's ourselves we mourn.

Casinos, fast food, vodka, and righteous scorn—
it is because we love you you don't exist,
a sign we love you, beloved never-born.

Warm darkness from which you were untimely torn—
better to be unborn than unloved, unkissed,
unknown—it isn't you but ourselves we mourn.

Some billboards here say simply JESUS or warn
of the many pleasant sins we must resist.
This sign says *Love your babies, born and unborn,*

as if this life weren't hell enough, the forlorn
and loveless driving from disappointing trysts
or to crappy jobs—it's only ourselves we mourn.

The giant Jesus weeps in his bloody thorns,
but rather than make us crash or slash our wrists
we sing our love to you, our lost unborn
and ourselves, the ones you've left, the ones we mourn.

CENTIPEDES

I used to fold clothes or wash the dishes
while talking on the phone, but recently
I started hunting centipedes. It's hard
to give anyone my full attention,
especially when that person is an ex—
besides, the house has grown infested.
Although some mornings I'll find one in my shoe,
the centipedes come out mostly at night.
When I turn on the hall light to go upstairs,
half a dozen, large and primordial,
will be clinging to the wall, and I always
grab a wad of tissue as I go
so I can squash them on my way to bed.

The first time I killed one I was shocked.
I barely touched the thing—it exploded
into a hundred little pieces of writhing
segments, antennae, and quivering legs.
How, I wondered, could such fragile creatures
survive to spawn countless generations?
At the top of the stairs I drop the bundle
in the toilet and watch the tissue unfold,
spilling centipieces into the water.
Sometimes I miss, and it drifts slowly down
the stairwell, long legs like parachute cords.
Three months after we bought this house, my ex
moved out, partly because of the centipedes.

On a good night I squash ten. The worst
was when I came upstairs and found one on
my toothbrush. Now each time I brush, I think
of bug legs bristling between my teeth.
I don't know where the centipedes come from.
There could be nests behind the floorboards, walls,
and ceilings. They could crawl in from the alley.
Sometimes I think they grow out of the fur
Otis sheds all over the house. It clumps
in corners, the same color and wispiness
as the centipedes. Autumn breezes come
and twist the hairs into little bundles,
breathing into them their primeval life.

Yesterday I saw three of my exes.
I dropped off our daughter at my ex-
wife's house, had lunch with a recent ex,
and last evening, as married people want
the whole world married, I went on a blind
date with a married couple and their friend.
Everything was going fine until
I saw across the restaurant an ex
I still love but who won't even speak to me.
She was having dinner with someone
she obviously loved. She was so absorbed
in him she didn't notice us as they left
and he chivalrously helped her with her jacket.

Home, drunk, a bad first and last
impression, too much Chianti, I forgot
to grab a wad of paper on my way
upstairs, and turned on the bedroom light
to hundreds of centipedes, assorted sizes,
scattered across my newly-painted white
ceiling—a starry sky in negative.
I lay in bed, spinning slowly, watching
them watch me back with their tiny black
unblinking eyes, before I finally
stood up swaying, dipping on my old
spongy mattress, fresh roll of toilet paper
in hand, hardly knowing where to start.

DOG DAYS

The season tires. The grass can grow no more.
Hard green tomatoes lack the heart to sweeten
while green beans brown and shrivel up uneaten.
The heat won't break. Even breathing's a chore.
Home from work, nothing has stirred here since
I left this morning. For my old dog Otis
it's as much an effort to get up and piss
as for me to watch him hobble to the fence.
Come on, old buddy, let us climb the stairs
to bed, a plate of leftovers, some required
reading on my chest. Let the moonlight creep
over our dirty dishes, laundry—who cares.
Let the crickets ratchet down the day and, tired,
the same old sentence lull us at last to sleep.

T W O

FIVE SONGS FOR HIDDEN PLACES

1. Song for the Cool Spot of my Pillow

My bathroom sink is broken—
leaks quarts a day of water.
The toilet's whine has woken
my sleeping baby daughter.

My mower broke—a bummer,
I've got it now up-ended.
My marriage broke last summer.
That's one I don't want mended.

My rear-view mirror broke off.
My side-view mirror cracked.
Is this just a smoker's cough?
I guess I won't look back.

I won a poetry prize—
200 bucks, not much.
This week the money flies
straight to my broken clutch.

The truth has broken through
the silence like a joke.
My heart is broken, too.
And I'm, of course, flat broke.

There's so much left unspoken
my voice breaks. Water seeps.

My bathroom sink is broken.
It crests as I drift to sleep.

2. Matchbook Song

A spark can burn the whole house down,
a match could raze a city block.
A book will set the whole damn town
in flames as fast as talk.

A drop could drown a butterfly,
a cup could drown a basement mouse.
Rain from an early April sky
steams off the roof of our house.

3. Back of a Beer Label

Sunday morning, drunk again,
the rain steams off the porch.
The worms crawl out, the dog wants in,
I hear the Baptist church.

This steaming April baptism
of life with you long gone—
I call and hear your cynicism
contagious as a yawn.

Oh, we lived and loved like man and wife,
then one of us had to move it,
but women like you come once in life—
I'll go through dozens to prove it.

4. Back Alley Song

When bars begin to close,
the lovers fall on my lawn—
night sewn tight by mosquitoes
beneath the brewery's neon,
and all the stars above
swept clean by city lights.
The lovers make drunk love
against the summer night,
as if they had time squirreled
safely and away,
then sleep until the world
spits out another day
while a life begins to grow
in the moon's dim undertow.

5. Solitary Drinking Song

Surrounded by our bed of weeds
that thrive in the shade of Jesus Church,
I take in the night and Rolling Rocks
out on my sagging wooden porch,
observe life's little consequences
through the chinks in wooden fences.
The sirens trigger barking dogs.
The brewery boils its cereal,
the steam making the neighborhood
yeasty and ethereal.
A helicopter sweeps the sky,
its spotlight sifting right from wrong.
The wind blows over my empty bottles
and sets the nothingness to song.

HOME

I like my hometown more
the longer I'm away.
Memories, like trick candles,
flicker as I pull in.

The longer I've been away
the less I recognize. Stars
flicker as I pull in.
Where are the woods and fields?

I barely recognize the stars.
Home is where
my boyhood woods and fields
now offer beautiful new homes.

Home is where they said
Leave now so we might miss you someday.
The beautiful new homes say
We're better off since you left.

We might miss you someday—
yes, that would be my wish.
Home is where they're better off since you left.
Blow into town and blow right out.

Yes, that would be my wish—
that I liked my hometown more.
Blow through town. Blow out
memories like trick candles.

DELAY

He sat on the porch, sipped his can of Stroh's.
Dinner's ready! He delayed coming inside.
Instead he looked over the rows and rows
of houses, contemplated stars that died
eons ago but only now reached him.
After the third call, he grabbed another
beer and moved into the dining room,
sat down among his children and their mother.
That night, when the kids slept, tempers would flare.
For now they had sloppy joes and Tater Tots.
They had leftovers in tight-lipped Tupperware,
and so they chose to savor this small draught
of calm, so cool and bland but also stable,
and flash dead smiles across the dinner table.

CHURCH

We were a pack of 8th grade boys,
and the whole world slept unawares.
A few weeks before summer break,
someone's older brother bought us
a case of Stroh's, which we took turns
carrying fullback-style down
dark ditches, through picket-fenced yards,
ducking what we thought were police
headlights combing trees, then ran
across our school's unlit playground,
where we lollygagged a bit,
big bad kids on little kids' toys,
then left to soap obscenities
on doors and windows of those girls
who teased then denied us everything,
most of the girls in the 8th grade class.
We tossed toilet paper in trees,
and being boys teeming with beer,
we gilded dozens of mailboxes
and porches. On the way back to our street,
we cut through the old church yard
and someone tried the door—unlocked!
We streamed in like orcs at the breach,
soaping the lower stained glass windows
and breaking candlesticks. Steve Mills
pissed in a bronze altar cup.
Jimmy Tosti, who was Catholic
and one of the worst students at school,
soaped "Fuck Gesus!" on the altar.

I watched my schoolmates go to work
and knew that many of these boys
were in the crowd that circled me
a year or two ago and told me
I was going to hell because
I wasn't baptized, and all were in
our social studies class the day
that everyone, including our teacher,
professed their faith in god and Jesus
except for me, and told me yet
again that I would burn in hell.
I don't want to portray myself
as some earnest teenage martyr
or atheistic saint, but I knew
the difference between right and wrong
and very wrong. No one saw me
leave the church, trot down the hill,
past the old cemetery plot
and through the little patch of woods
thick with poison ivy and kudzu,
the sounds of crashing benches and laughing
teenage boys swallowed by darkness.
I finally made it to my own
front porch. The neighborhood was dark
and quiet. The Roysters' tabby slinked
beneath the streetlight, a few crickets
chirped in the shrubs, and I had the beer.

Sweet November

Each of us sniffing, the dog and I cross
warm laundry smells, wafts of dinners finished
hours ago, and the corner pub's last calls,
and there I see her through the moon-glossed window.
Decorously slow, she is undressing,
shedding all except her underwear
and the soft blue light from her television.
I know this is wrong but can't tear myself
away, and Otis happily marks his turf
on a small heap of leaves, and she reaches up,
lingers, half slipping out of silhouette
as she pulls something from a dark shelf.
I feel like a creep. Otis tugs to go,
and though I won't realize it till after
I get home tonight, this, or something
like it, is why I went on my late walk.
The girl crosses the room to her TV
and then the world goes black. Perhaps she sees me,
awkward in her window. Perhaps she reaches
for the phone—or smiles, knowing she is safe
in her darkness, door locked against the outside,
where the wind rustles scraps of leaves, nudging
me home on gusts of November's sweet decay.

HORSE

"Well, I'm gonna get a horse," Ken tells me.
I hadn't heard him lumber up the alley,
startling me in the middle of my shot.
The sun glints off his balding head, dimpled
and scarred on one side, eyes piggishly close.
He says, "How 'bout a rematch?" We play horse.
Ken hurls the basketball like I imagine
Polyphemus hurling boulders. His shots
land nowhere near the backboard, over the fence
and bushes, deep in my unmowed yard of weeds.
"You got your horse all picked out?" I ask.
"Go this week to make sure. It's a palomino!"

Last summer I was changing a punctured tire
in the driveway. Ken saw me working, came out
and said, "Well, I'm going to Daytona.
Got a job working on stock car crew."
"That's great, Ken," I said, like a proud big brother.
"I haven't worked since 1978,"
he said, and this part may be true.
One spring he saw me washing my old Mustang,
said he just came back from the Botanical Gardens
where he'd tried to get some women's phone numbers.
"I can't help but notice you've had some luck
with the ladies. You got any advice for me?"
"Oh, I've had plenty of bad luck, too," I said.
"Once I was dating this Playboy Bunny,"
he said. "She sure showed me a thing or two!"
Ken laughed, his whole face scrunching like a rag.

Retrieving boulders from over the fence,
I happen to look up and catch my girlfriend's
shadow in the window as she watches
us play. I figure she's still mad at me.
Finally, Ken spells out horse. "Well, Ken,
I'd better get cleaned up and go to work,"
I lie, wondering which is more plausible—
my lies to him, his lies to me, my acting
like I believe his lies, or the lies that might
have made life easier if we had told them.
At last Ken goes inside. I play a little
fast-paced one-on-zero, my jumpers clanging
and clanging off the rim, my rhythm off
until I dribble out to the alley, split
a double team and sink a last second shot
beyond the arc. Swish. Easy. Keep shooting.

SOULARD MARDI GRAS ROUND

"Jesus had a huge impact on Christianity,"
one of my composition students writes.
Two days after Soulard Mardi Gras
plastic beer cups topple down the street.
After lunch my stomach acid begins to gnaw.
Plastic beads lie on my girlfriend's vanity.
Blue Port-a-Potties steam on every corner
two days after Soulard Mardi Gras.

One of my composition students writes,
"Leave her lie where Jesus flang her!"
Reelect Ken Ortman your Soulard Alderman.
Stomach acid gnaws. A siren grows louder.
From the tower of Saints Peter and Paul
one can see, over the brewery, a cemetery—
the town's shadow lengthening toward night.
Plastic beer cups gather in doorways.

"Leave her lie where Jesus flang her!"
The town's shadow lengthens toward night.
A Port-a-Potty steams on the corner
of Saints Peter and Paul. A siren grows louder.
Two days after Mardi Gras, on the vanity,
plastic beads slink between lotions and powders.
One of my composition students writes,
"Jesus had a huge impact on Christianity."

INSESTINA

"Is this some terrible trend?" our young new
assistant editor asked. "All these incest
poems and stories sent for our next issue!"
It's older than Oedipus, I thought, shocking
as Electra, these forbidden family
secrets that should have remained private,

those dark places people put their privates,
as if we could possibly put them someplace new.
Even sex with those not strictly family
(step-siblings, in-laws) glistens with that incestuous
thrill, boy-meets-girl with extra shock,
these kids towing U-hauls of family issues.

At some point, though, I feel I must take issue.
The personal needn't bleed into the private.
After years in the biz, it doesn't shock.
As if to make it deep and dark and new
we need to lace a work with themes of incest,
but no matter how screwed up our families,

it doesn't mean we have to screw our families
and hock like shiny trinkets our shabby issues.
We succumb to that tempting strain of incest,
as if so great a theme frees us from our private
little angsts, as if the merely true or new
makes Great Art or rescues us from shock-

therapy. Sometimes the stories transcend shock
when those same recycled genes kept in the family
for generations create some monstrous new
species—the mutant DNA that issues
from the loins and then gets shut in private
rooms or attics. Oh, but enough of incest.

This business is already too incestuous.
That editors publish our friends (oh shock!)
who are also editors, who in our private
hours spend time with each others' families,
and then turn up in one another's issues,
should hardly come as something new.

So send to our upcoming issue: make it shock like new,
make privates public if you must, but, please,
if you insist on incest, keep it in the family.

BLESS THEIR HEARTS

At Steak 'n Shake I learned that if you add
"Bless their hearts" after their names, you can say
whatever you want about them and it's OK.
My son, bless his heart, is an idiot,
she said. *He rents storage space for his kids'*
toys–they're only one and three years old!
I said, *my father, bless his heart, has turned*
into a sentimental old fool. He gets
weepy when he hears my daughter's greeting
on our voice mail. Before our Steakburgers came
someone else blessed her office mate's heart,
then, as an afterthought, the jealous hearts
of the entire anthropology department.
We bestowed blessings on many a heart
that day. I even blessed my ex-wife's heart.
Our waiter, bless his heart, would not be getting
much tip, for which, no doubt, he'd bless our hearts.
In a week it would be Thanksgiving,
and we would each sit with our respective
families, counting our blessings and blessing
the hearts of family members as only family
does best. Oh, bless us all, yes, bless us, please
bless us and bless our crummy little hearts.

MAY ALL YOUR CHRISTMASES
BE WHITE-KNUCKLED

The sewer backs up right under us downstairs—
with every flush it gargles thick black water.
The table's decked with candles, silverware,

wedding crystal, and the tablecloth they bought her.
But fancy can't gloss over the forced smiles,
the fact I'm not what they hoped for their daughter.

We eat in silence, pretend we don't hear the bile
my ex-wife spills out loudly over the phone,
as I contemplate the cons and cons awhile:

to be miserable together or alone?
The company includes me unawares—
we pick the carcass down to the bitter bone,

together swallowing our oaths and prayers,
while the sewer backs up under us downstairs.

THREE

THE ARTISTS

After the painting A Gallant Musical Pause at Delft,
1674, by Jan Verkolje (Dutch, 1650-1693)

The courtly neighbor, music teacher, family friend,
perhaps distant cousin, turns from his spinet,

gestures to the svelte viol de gamba
with his right hand, while the young bride's grip loosens

from the long neck of her cittern. Above them,
in a picture, gold-framed, over the mantel,

an amorous couple blurs themselves to oblivion.
Across the room, to her left, his many-feathered hat

slinks over a chair, and a spaniel,
that dogged symbol of fidelity,

sniffs at him suspiciously from the rug's edge.
Her husband must be overseas, his war banner

slumped into itself, but she stands—after this
courtly crescendo, the frenzied grace notes—unfurled

and her white ruffles billow, tell us, my love,
that no love, not even illicit, is ever wrong.

And though this gallant musical pause
may not, in courtiers' eyes, be so gallant,

and her husband will soon return as hero,
their hands clasp at the center of the canvas—

a fermata held however indefinitely,
held at the sole discretion of the artists.

Two Lullabies

1. After Drinking

Come lie with me close, my love,
and calm your shivering sobs.
Tomorrow we'll rise comatose
to work our stupid jobs.

Your necklace spills on the vanity,
my boots kick off with a clunk,
so come fall into bed with me
and let's sleep off this drunk.

Let's part the curtains, lift the blinds,
let moonlight quell this storm.
Come lie beside me, close your eyes—
our bed is once more warm.

Let's hold each other in tight arms
to keep the world from spinning.
The morning sun will sift through blinds—
another new beginning.

Your loveliness will long outlast
my decaying eyesight,
though who'd drink in as recklessly
your tear-streaked face in streetlight?

For loving others is as much
warm hearts and warmer kisses

as taking a cold-eyed, ruthless gaze
at our own weaknesses.

So dry your sorrows with our sheets,
hang troubles on the bed knobs,
and come lie with me close, my love,
and I will calm your sobs.

2. Falling Asleep

For years now as I've lain me down to sleep,
I've patted down my mind as well as my bed,
picking one thought to think while falling asleep—
yes, the lovely women I'd love to bed,
but also problem poems, problems at work

to mull over before and during sleep.
Tonight, I lie here alone. Nothing works.
Nothing is further away than you and sleep,
no favorite dream to nurse and then dream.

Mist thickens to rain as summer turns to fall.
What a beautiful little dream we dreamed.
I lie in bed and think of nothing, then fall

asleep listening to the wind and rain
sounding like nothing but the wind and rain.

FUGUE IN COLD AND RAIN

The sky rains cold and black,
this porch my only haven.
Inside the furnace lurches
and shakes like a heart attack.
At least three days unshaven,
I've swilled Merlot since two.
Black clouds swoop and swallow
the spires of red-brick churches.
The sky rains cold and black.
Nothing good will follow.
Wet leaves hiss like a curse,
and at my worst, I confess:
my own black rains are worse.
The wet winds lash and break
the surface of the pond
in the park across the street.
My only warmth is you—
what you gain is beyond
what I can hope to guess.
It rains down in black sheets.
The furnace shivers—I shake,
watch trash whip down the alley.
The wind won't be consoled
but can't work up a finale.
The sky rains black and cold.

FLOOD WATCH

The heavens must have saved up all their worst
for this night after two straight months of storms.
Thunder bumps off a row of car alarms,
the rain rains off our gutters, and each burst
of lightning pastes itself for several seconds
inside our eyelids. Even the pond fish float
waterlogged. Soon they'll issue us a lifeboat—
so at least our next door neighbor reckons.
We crouch half-sheltered on the steps out front.
The river licks the levee yet we want
for nothing, our candy down from the top shelves.
We've worked all year and paid most of our debts,
holding clammy hands and killing ourselves
with Claret, Scotch, and glowing cigarettes.

WHILE YOU WERE AWAY . . .

I thought about sex. I turned 40, drank beer
on the back porch by myself. Called an ex.
Last night, the woman across the alley, the one
with that green porch light, suddenly appeared
in a white-and-black Dalmatian-spotted bathrobe,
bare legs, and slippers and shuffled down the alley.
She may have seen me, but she also saw
our other neighbor's Datsun gone, that guy
she dated once or twice, out all night,
and so she quickly shuffled right back home.
Her dog sniffed disdainfully from the porch,
for once refused to come down into the yard.
From the front side of the house, across the street,
a guy kept yelling, "April! April! April!"
He pounded on the door, "C'mon, April!"
I am also sick of the month of March.
The season sucks us out of houses, pulls
us onto porches and down damp alleys. We keep
testing our breaths against the cool night air.

This afternoon I made corn chowder, baked bread,
roasted asparagus for that family of three,
the mother with ovarian cancer now
for the second time. Her ten-year-old daughter
plays sweeper on the fourth-grade soccer team.
I wonder if the couple still has sex,
and if they do each time feels like the last.

Tonight the neighborhood is quiet.

No dogs bark. Everyone must have been
sucked back inside, maybe licking their wounds.
Our neighbor's light still burns a fungus green.
The roots begin to stir in the cold March rain.
I feel like I've been 40 all my life.
My daughter is at her mother's, and tonight,
you are so much further away than sleep.
I finish another six-pack, go upstairs
and crawl beneath the covers, shiver, naked.
The dog's been on the bed, smelly but warm—
the only warmth tonight, so I'll take it.

LESSONS FROM THE GARDEN

This morning little mushroom heads,
like rusted dimes on toothpick stalks,
sprang up in our flower box.
An hour later they were dead,

withered in the summer heat.
Each spore stretched out its mortal coil
through dried-up peat and city soil
to die upon a slab of concrete.

With mouthless moths and butterflies,
the male flies free, no need for food,
and mates to spawn a hungry brood
then lives another hour and dies,

unable even to watch its spawn
chew my tomatoes to the ground.
If they had mouths their song would sound
pointless, pointless over the lawn.

Inside, my daughter's forced to practice.
Her fingers blunder down the keys,
ignoring accidentals. She's
thirteen, more prickly than a cactus.

Outside the yard is newly mown—
I hear the chirps of brazen birds,
wrong notes accented by swear words,
and realize lately how she's grown

almost as moody as my ex-wife.
A year ago she loved to play.
She hates it now and pounds away
a stubborn song of loss and life.

GIFTS

Last night I played a terrible game, missed all
my open shots, dribbled off my foot, even
passed the ball to a guy on the other team.
Three days a week we play in a dusky gym
with half the lights burnt out—half of us
burnt out as well though every now and then
someone will catch fire and play untouchable
to the rest of us a few flickering moments,
and every week I remember Bo, who,
at seven feet and blessed with outside range,
had no desire to play college hoop.
The kid was also born with perfect pitch,
an All-State drummer and percussionist,
but after graduating Central High
he chose to go to engineering school
near home so he could get a decent job.
Such gifts wasted on the unimaginative!
That height and grace and shooting and no passion
for the game. And perfect pitch wasted on
a percussionist! Bo only wanted to work
all week and play REO Speedwagon
in a refinished basement on weekends.
My own fires must be fueled by lack of gifts.
For fifteen years I flailed around in bands,
blasting out my modestly talented ears,
crisscrossing the Midwest but going nowhere.
At 41 I still can't dribble or shoot
but those three days a week I trip up and down
the court on rolled ankles and shot knees,

grip that ball in my jammed and crooked fingers.
Oh, how I wanted to be a star
on court or stage. Sometimes I think the most
considerate gift of all might be not trying
to make the most of our modest gifts, instead
collapsing back into the dark matter
that comprises most of us so as to let
the real stars shine brighter. Of course last night,
none of our flames burned longer than the squeak
from shoes—but even game played badly is
more fun than no game. We lock the outside doors
so no one has to watch, and our aging bodies
collect the most exuberant bruises.
Desire outpaces talent down the court
to flub a lay-up, our hopeful three-pointers
and self-mockery and teasing laughter
floating like scraps of song among the rafters.

THE WHITE BUS OF FAILURE

Once a school bus, CHURCH OF THE NAZARENE
now bleeds through its layers of latex paint.
Stained glass decals peel from every window.

He'd wrestled its transmission since last April,
sheaf of weathered parking tickets stuffed
behind a wiper like a yellow bouquet.

We've never seen his face, but several times
while walking the dog we have witnessed legs
stuck out from under his obsolete machine

next to a greasy cardboard box of tools.
Last summer, once, he left the back door open,
revealing carpet, woodwork, furniture—

a movable living room that never moves.
Its oil stains outpace it down the street.
October, we shift the day an hour to no

effect—the days grow shorter, darker faster.
At dinner hour we hear him from across
the vacant lot, clanging, cursing the dark.

If we were praying people, we would pray.
Instead we hope for him, though more for us,
this hope that drives us through our dying days.

DUMPSTER FIRES

We'd been working late and were overtired
as we walked down the stairs, stepped into the night,
and failed at first to notice the dumpster fires

burning their orange and reddish dawn-like light.
A fire burned at every block, leading
into neighborhoods no suburbanite

would enter even by day, the flames feeding
off office trash and shipping boxes. A squad
of firemen pulled up, red lights bleeding,

while shadows flapped and fluttered against facades,
a tarantella of reds and blacks. Such blood-stained
beauty in such burning rage made us applaud—

a rage that burned no less useless, contained—
and as we drove back home, the sky fell. It rained.

December Evening

A shitty day at work, I come home tired
to fix dinner for my hungry daughter:
the fastest—mac & cheese. I boil the water,
look out the kitchen window at phone wires
cutting across the sky, gray and thick
as curdled milk, the rows and rows of boarded
up homes, the brewery chimneys blowing sordid
smells, the alley piles of scabby bricks,
a landscape so man-made it's inhumane.
On many evenings such as these I've thought
how only when we're too tired and strained
to feel it can we truly call it love,
and so I drain the noodles, return the pot
to the orange coils of sunset on my stove.

COMMUNION

This cold January morning, the moon
melts in the sky like a communion wafer
above St. Peter's Episcopal Church
cattycorner from my daughter's school,
and idling in the drop-off line, I recall
how as a child I sometimes took communion,
cared nothing for the blood and bones of Christ
but wanted terribly to taste the wine
administered by Father Wyatt, who wiped
our spit from the chalice with his silky cloth.
Our St. Paul's Father left his red-trimmed robes,
his wife and kids, left town, too—we soon learned
he'd married someone from our congregation.
I look through the long line of windshields
at all the tired faces behind the wheels,
our cars fuming ghostly white exhaust,
think *we can never guess who'll stay in line
or who'll drop out*, but I am still in line,
a bit slow from two bottles of Bordeaux,
the night's back porch communion with my wife,
and I can smell my vices through my pores
and wonder if my daughter can as well,
wonder how many other parents feel
hung-over, feel like bolting, dragging themselves
through hours spent on nothing more than money,
but now, this morning, here we are once more,
the sunlight gleaming from thrown-open doors,
the frost retracting up windshields, the moon
dissolving in January's pale blue spit.

When Men Stopped Wearing Hats, When Women Stopped Wearing Gloves

Little impulse, little nod,
a little sweat drying on the brow.
A woman's fingers strain
to run through his hair like shy deer.
He leans forward while she caresses
the little coves where the hair recedes.
Cells glide over cells,
and all the other cells roar their approval.
What more have they hoped for than this
little dance, a little naked grace
beyond the tug and bind of our stitches.
All this for us, that we may sit close in moonlight,
restless as two strangers, exchanging
our wild gifts, my head in your hands.

LITTLE FUGUE OF LOVE AND DEATH

We talked of the end of the world and then
We sang us a song, and then sang it again.
        —Woody Guthrie, "This Dusty Old Dust"

The sky is gray. My joints are old.
The terrorists will nuke us.
I cannot shake this summer cold.
My head's a hive of mucous.

Our dog is old. He cannot shake.
He collapses in the iris.
Dead birds litter the alleyway,
a wave of West Nile virus.

We drink beneath the new flight path
the clouds can't hope to deaden.
We can't see T-birds, Raptors, Blackhawks,
but it sounds like Armageddon.

And you and I sit on our porch,
drenched head to toe in Deet.
We swill the High Life, holding hands
despite the record heat.

The dog has grayed. The sky has grayed.
The grass and shrubs have browned.
Our life is high. The sky is low.
Our love goes round and round.

ACKNOWLEDGMENTS

Grateful acknowledgment is made to the following magazines where these poems first appeared:

Boulevard: "Five Songs for Hidden Places," "Domestic Fugues," "Sweet November," and "Fugue in Cold and Rain" and "Little Song of Love and Death" (published as "Two Fugues")

Crab Orchard Review: "Bless Their Hearts," "Church," "Home"

Flyway: "Wharf Ruins"

52nd City: "Horse"

Locuspoint: "Insestina," "May All Your Christmases Be White-Knuckled"

The Louisville Review: "The Artists," "Dumpster Fires," "Lessons from the Garden"

The Melic Review: "The Unborn"

New Letters: "Old Bird"

Pleiades: "The Final Fuck"

Poetry East: "Gifts"

Seattle Review: "December Evening"

Southern Poetry Review: "White Bus of Failure"

The Sun: "When Men Stopped Wearing Hats, When Women Stopped Wearing Gloves," "While You Were Away..."

Tar River Poetry: "Man Drives with Shark Attached to Leg," "Soulard Mardi Gras Round"

32 Poems: "Dog Days"

Unsplendid: "Two Lullabies" (section 2, "Falling Asleep")

"Old Bird" was selected for the *New Letters* 2007 Readers Choice Award. "Bless Their Hearts" and "Home" also appeared on *Verse Daily*. "Bless Their Hearts and "While You Were Away . . ." also appeared in the anthology *Seriously Funny: Poems About Love, God, War, Art, Sex, Madness, and Everything Else* (University of Georgia Press, 2009). Many of these poems also appeared in the chapbook *24 Tall Boys: Dark Verse for Light Times* (Snark Publishing/Firecracker Press, 2007). "Delay" appeared in *World's Not Fair: An Anthology of St. Louis Poets* (Walrus Publishing, 2009). "December Evening" originally appeared in *Borrowed Towns* (Word Press, 2005).

I would like to thank my dearest wife and daughter, my parents and Ricki, my basketball homies, Scott Berman, The Cat's Meow, Richard Cecil, Kathleen Driskell, Karen Duffy, Madeleine Morgan Fentress, Tom C. Hunley, Kara's Grandma, KFMers of yore (Cathy Carlisi, Bill Coyle, Chelsea Rathburn, and Catherine Tufariello), Erin Keane, Aimee Levitt, Joanne Lowery, Mike Martin and the Writing Center, Molly McCaffrey, Keith and Cathy Moyer, Otis (may he snore in peace), Molly Peacock, *The Riverfront Times*, the *River Styx* board and staff, Alan Shapiro, Snark Publishing, Jim Sodon and the St. Louis Community College English Department, The Speed Art Museum in Louisville, Maura Stanton, and Uncle Larry.

RICHARD NEWMAN is the author of the poetry collection *Borrowed Towns* (Word Press, 2005) and several poetry chapbooks, including *24 Tall Boys: Dark Verse for Light Times* (Snark Publishing/Firecracker Press, 2007) and *Monster Gallery: 19 Terrifying and Amazing Monster Sonnets!* (Snark Publishing, 2005). His poems have appeared in *Best American Poetry, Boulevard, Crab Orchard Review, Poetry Daily, The Sun, Tar River Poetry, Verse Daily,* and many other periodicals and anthologies. He lives with his wife and daughter in St. Louis, where he teaches at St. Louis Community College, edits *River Styx,* and co-directs the River Styx at Duff's Reading Series.

CPSIA information can be obtained at www.ICGtesting.com
Printed in the USA
BVOW07s1441061013

333028BV00014B/279/P

9 780982 416914